The Cry of
Another Mother

The Cry of Another Mother

You're not alone

Felicia Noble

WESTBOW
PRESS®
A DIVISION OF THOMAS NELSON
& ZONDERVAN

WestBow Press books may be ordered through booksellers or by contacting:

WestBow Press
A Division of Thomas Nelson & Zondervan
1663 Liberty Drive
Bloomington, IN 47403
www.westbowpress.com
844-714-3454

ISBN: 978-1-5127-5508-4 (sc)
ISBN: 978-1-5127-5509-1 (hc)
ISBN: 978-1-5127-5507-7 (e)

Library of Congress Control Number: 2016914156

Print information available on the last page.

WestBow Press rev. date: 05/06/2021

Contents

Contents

About the Author

For several years, Felicia Noble has inspired friends and family on effective ways to cope with life's unforeseen obstacles and everyday decision making. That might sound simple to many of you, but it's challenging to others. Felicia has faced many trials and tribulations; she has carried the burdens of others as they shared their stories with her, but she continues to be a productive person in a world of unexpected, life changing dangers.

In my opinion, she has earned the title Storm Catcher. Through it all, she has remained confident and sane knowing that her painful tragedy has an indefinite power of its own. She would agree with many by saying "It's God who holds all the answers to every circumstance." Though she has experienced a tragic loss, her smile shines on.

Her sense of humor is contagious. Many people ask her opinions when they're afflicted by life's trials and tribulations. She's always willing to listen and respond in a manner that would leave the recipient satisfied if he or she could accept her truth.

After she lost her son to gun violence, she decided it was time to help others who have suffered such losses through her words and the guidance of the Holy Spirit. She knows the pain that mothers who lose their children to violence feel. It is evident by the senseless murders in the communities and the world. She believes her story will help others cope with tragedy… perhaps without cause. She acknowledged that "mothers" are in pain and hope that her story will help someone.

Note for Back of Book

The *Cry of Another Mother* is a personal story of a mother's ultimate challenge—coping with the murder of her son and how she continued to live while healing. Her battle has been ongoing, yet her strength continues to be triumphant with the comfort of knowing she's empowered by a strength greater than herself. In her heart, she trusts she has been chosen by God to reach out to those who have been directly or indirectly affected by the death of a loved one.

This is a must-read. The author is not just telling her story; she also engages with the reader. She reaches out to her audience to embrace and reassure them that they are not alone in life's storms (trials and tribulations); she has been there. Some have been unknowingly challenged with teenage pregnancy, broken relationships, and physical or mental abuse. Many are all too familiar with trials and tribulations and feeling overwhelmed and unprepared because they have not learned the power of faith and prayer.

The writer shares her heartfelt story with her audience so they too can become strong at times when they think they're weak.

For several years, Felicia Noble has inspired friends and family on effective ways to cope with life's difficult and unforeseen challenges. Many refer to these challenges as life's storms. After many storms in her life, she was always able to bounce back, but this time was different. This novel was written and inspired by the remembrance of her firstborn and only son, Damond, a.k.a. "Mr. Face" Harris.

Chapter *1*

Denial

I was sitting in my living room looking out the window at 4:00 a.m., into the dawn of day. I was usually not awake at that hour, but I hadn't slept in days. That day was different from others. I couldn't put my finger on it, mostly because I was in denial. Who wouldn't have been? After all I'd been through that week alone, it was amazing that I was still standing. I was filled with anxiety.

Mentally I was exhausted, all I could remember was falling to my knees surrounded by colorless walls, unmatched chairs, and faceless staff all in white lab coats in a hospital waiting room, looking for me. It hadn't been to pray this time; I fell to my knees in disbelief. What on earth was I doing there on that summer day. I usually only came for a few things: good music, good food and endless shopping. Nothing more nothing less, period.

I couldn't stand up. I felt weak, limp. I could hardly speak, and hearing was totally out of the question. Listen to what more of what? More details of what I hoped was not true? Slap me I must have been asleep. I had so much on my mind, thoughts blocked by the crack in my heart. I was stressed and in shock. I'd felt that way ever since I had left Chicago.

Something deep down in my soul, told me things would never be the same again. I couldn't think clearly, a definite sign of mental trauma. I stuttered each spoken word that came from my mouth. Eyes fixed in my state of shock. Others on the receiving end of the conversation asked: "what's wrong, why are you talking like that." I didn't know, I seemed to no longer be me, I was the shell of what I used to be. I was confined to denial. I had always spoken clearly prior to April 20th, 2010. *Why can't I figure this out?* I asked myself. My mind was clouded. *What happened? A case of mistaken identity or simply a misunderstanding between strangers?*

That long and congested ride to the hospital had been a nightmare. The traffic from Milwaukee to Chicago was bumper to bumper. I turned to look at Patrick (as I yelled) you can't drive any faster. I thought you were from Chicago. I thought you knew where you were going. I could get there faster if I had walked, I stated. I must have sounded so mean but at the time I didn't care. I only wanted to reach my destination as soon as possible and get to my son.

I walked over to my son as he laid there. I filled a pink hospital basin with cold water and gently wiped dried blood from my son's cool face. I had to do something; my nursing skills kicked in. That was the last time I would be able to touch him. I mean everyone was just sitting, looking and doing nothing. His son (Javonni) paced the floor, thrashing his arms around. He cried out for his father with anger and pain. I could see mouths moving, some appeared to be ranting and raving. Others sat with their head hanging down, no I couldn't hear their voices in that moment it was me and him, my son.

A few of the on lookers appeared to cry without tears, faces dry as the desert. Others looked relieved, satisfied that he had succumb to his death. When I close my eyes, I can still see the abrasion on his forehead; he must have fallen and hit his head on the concrete after he was shot and killed. I envisioned how afraid he must have been as those bullets punctured his skin, one severing his femoral artery, smh (shaking my head.) I knew from his injuries that he bled out.

As the onlookers sat and did just that—looked—I bent over to my son's ear. I quietly spoke as my voice cracked and tears rolled down my cheek, as though he could hear me. I whispered my painful disbelief of him lying motionless on a gurney. The nurse had assured me that I wouldn't have to go to the morgue to see him. I said, "Mama's not mad at you". "Mama loves you." It's alright but it's not ok.". I kissed his forehead with tears in my eyes and unforgettable, unimaginable pain in my heart.

I tried to make sense of it—as if there were such a thing. All I knew to do was ask for help, hoping that my voice would be heard by God. With all the strength I had left, which wasn't much, I yelled, "Jesus! Please help me. You're my only refuge. Without you, whom do I have, and where do I go in this time of despair? Do I go to church on Sunday and request a miracle from you, Jesus, the miracle maker? Or do I stand in the middle of the floor and scream at the top of my lungs? Do I stomp my feet and demand to be given another of life's battles? Not this one, please, Jesus."

I begged for an answer. "Why Damond, my child? Why today?". Of course, I knew a different day would not have made it any better. I needed to muster up enough strength to perhaps ask one of the sisters, brothers, or our pastor to pray for me without ceasing. I asked myself, *Does prayer really work in any circumstance? Can it be compared to the mailman, who delivers rain or shine?*

A very dear friend who has now gone on to be with the Lord once told me that when you can't change a situation or you don't know what to say regarding a problem, just call upon the name of Jesus. I was calling with my hands raised; I wouldn't and couldn't believe any of this. I didn't care what the doctor had already confirmed; he could have been wrong. We must have had a bad connection. "Hello, Jesus, can you hear me now? Am I yelling loud enough? Could this be the one time you've made a mistake? Jesus, as difficult as it is to say and sometimes accept, I know you make no mistakes because you're the only perfect one. There is no one greater than you." I know that our life's journey was written before ?we were formed in our mother's womb.

I couldn't decide what to think about first. Move forward forgetting everything that had hurt me? Why bother to think about anything at all? That was it. I was going to tell myself that all was good—no worries, no cares. I decided to just cover my head with my blanket and not think or perhaps not remember anything at all. It seemed easier that way. I wanted to sleep, but that was impossible. I screamed in my pillow so I wouldn't wake up others in the house. My mother, grandmother and others had traveled from Mississippi to offer support while dealing with the pain of our loss.

I lay on the sofa with my eyes closed, but my eyelids were transparent. I saw it all—the good, the bad, and the ugly. What I couldn't see, my heart could feel—all the pain of that terrible day, the day my life seemed to stop and everything else ceased to matter.

If what they say is true, I can believe what I see. *But what if I don't want to see? What causes me to cry endlessly? What went wrong that day? Was someone mad, or … naw. Did someone other than me get up on the wrong side of the bed?* I couldn't believe after experiencing the greatest pain in my life that I was still among the living. It seemed it would be much easier for me to just give up, surrender to the pain. Many others would have. So why should I have been any different? "Lord, please give me one reason to continue living." I screamed, "Jesus! Help me!" I pressed my face against my hands to silence my cry. I felt as though I couldn't breathe. I was filled with such anxiety, which made me cry louder and harder. I tried to compose myself but couldn't. *Am I dreaming, or am I really awake?* I dropped my head in disbelief as I looked at the dawn of the day.

Something was missing. It just didn't seem real. I didn't feel whole that day. A big, important piece of me was missing. *Please someone, shake me if this is my reality, I don't want any part of it.* Leaving the hospital without my son was so hard.

Talking to the detectives was a real out of body experience. As I was being questioned, I became stolic, appearing unaffected. That couldn't have been further from the truth. My mind and heart were in big trouble.

The only anchors I had in that battle were my soul and the blood of Jesus.

The only ones awake in my house were Jesus, me, and my dog, Isaiah. People often say a dog is one's best friend. I considered Isaiah mine. He was always available, rendering no curfew on the length or content of that painful conversation. He seemed to know my mood without my having said anything or having made any gesture.

When I moved to a different room, he followed. When my days were good, he'd wag his tail and jump all around. When my days were bad, he wouldn't let me out of his sight. He is so overprotective. I didn't know how he knew my every temperament, but he did. I was happy for his unconditional love, not knowing how much I needed it.

He became my best friend after the experience of many trials and tribulations in my life and the many sorrowful stories shared by friends. A good friend shared with me about her stormy marriage to the man of her dreams, tall, good looking and charming. She would say, "All without cause or human solutions." Just when it seemed she was happy, it soon turned to sadness. She would often say, "I'm sharing my deepest pain with you. I want you to listen in detail to my experience of abuse so others can 'own' their afflicted abuse to heal.

(in her words) I can remember being punched and stomped in my head and on my body. I was bruised and in pain physically and mentally."

"What part of the game was that?" I asked her. "What would entice a man to harm a woman he says he loves?" I remembered her wearing sunglasses in the winter. She said it wasn't always due to the sunny days. It was because of the black eye she couldn't cover with makeup as she had times before. She did everything she could to keep any evidence of abuse from her three adult children, who were living their own lives. She said she didn't want them to know what she was going through. She said she loved him so much and didn't want her children to hate him.

It seemed clear to me that he didn't love her. I looked at her with her head hanging down. It reminded me of the new pain I had now and would forever feel; nothing could compare to that. Some children, especially sons, can be very overprotective as Isaiah was toward me. No one is good enough for their sisters and mother. I could only imagine what she must have been going through with her adult children. The children's love was priceless; they wouldn't have tolerated her being hurt physically or mentally by anyone. She said she wanted peace in her home. I witnessed her praying that everyone would just get along.

She expressed wanting so badly for her marriage to work out. She prayed that they would make it through that storm and be happy. As they were prior to whatever went wrong between them.

I listened to her stories of the physical and mental abuse. She and I shared our dreams of healthy relationships and family. We talked about our children and what type of parent we needed to be so that our children would follow in our positive footsteps.

Of course, parents always want children to have more of the good in life and less to none of what's bad. They are the apple of their mother's eye.

She was sure she had been ready for a long-term relationship like marriage that was a no-brainer. Although it too comes with real responsibility and imperfections that may accompany any relationship.

She cried out, "Perhaps he wasn't ready for a committed relationship." I think he treated her as though he hated her. But who was I to judge? My plate was over-flowing already. "She would say, "I didn't make him marry me". It was a mutual agreement, or so she thought." She looked deep into my eyes as though hoping, I had the answers she longed for.

She continued to say "I was afraid to talk to him because it seemed that almost anything would set him off. He has fought me for no reason at all. "There were many times I decided to agree to disagree, but that caused problems too." As women we must not waste valuable time on stagnant relationships.

I began to pray: *Lord, I know you hear the cries of your children. Who do we turn to in painful circumstances? How can people turn to others—friends, coworkers—without feeling ashamed or worthless?* I wanted to reassure her that I understood. She had confidence and trust in me and our friendship. I wanted her to know there was no need to be embarrassed or ashamed. "Please don't feel as though you've failed. God always leaves room in our lives for improvement.

There's no need to feel hopeless, powerless, unloved, or unwanted."

"You don't understand the pain of my abuse!" She said crying. "It happens without warning."

I reminded her to be thankful in all things, especially things we don't understand. I am not saying that abuse is ever ok. I am saying once the abuse has occurred. We must develop a plan to safely escape. "When two or more come together, Jesus is in their midst. Pray to Jesus, 'Thank you for your protection. Thank you for being the eyes that see and understand all when you can't see clearly.'" "Thank you" God, for my pain, so that I can be a blessing to others.

No one should suffer mental or physical abuse ever. It's much too painful to endure. There were times I felt so badly for her. At the time, it seemed that the pain would never end. It forced me to think of others who might have been suffering. I wanted to make other women and men aware that we have choices about what we'll take or not in stormy relationships.

My friend shared so many details of her relationship; I thank her for her trust in me. During one of our many phone conversations, I realized that when things didn't go his way, she would become the victim of circumstance. I knew she needed me to just be an ear.

"I hadn't done anything wrong to him," she told me. "I maintained my duties as a faithful and respectful wife: cooking, cleaning, intimacy, support, and open communication, or so I thought. During the few times there was a crisis in his family or with him, I was there but unnoticed. He seemed to lean on others for support, and that hurt her feelings which broke her heart. I never understood what happens between people. When it appears easy to hurt one another. Do we somehow get in the way of each other? Maybe many of us were two people in the wrong place at the wrong time."

Loving someone or being in love doesn't necessarily translate into a lasting, productive relationship. We must remember not to lose our identity. In battles, we must hold our heads up and wait for our breakthroughs, our blessings from the Lord. I also know can how it feels to be paralyzed with fear and afraid to fight back or defend oneself. Once you're physically or mentally damaged by someone else, it's easy to feel as though you're not good enough or it's your fault. But no one should feel as though he or she is in any battle alone. Jesus is always available any time, any place, for as long as you need him. No questions asked, without judgement.

I'm not perfect; Jesus is the only perfect one. Many times, we end up feeling unwanted, unworthy and afraid to leave an unhealthy relationship. I wanted to intervene, but I knew she had to vent. We must allow pain to run its course. She had to first, give herself permission to own her accountability, of the dysfunction before she could heal. She needed to realize no one should put up with abuse; no one is ever alone when he or she wants to safely walk away from it. The holy spirit is always with us, we can call out. Remembering obedience and our faith is what conquers pain.

She told me, "Once, I asked him, 'Why didn't you come home last night? I was awake most of the night. I was worried something had happened to you."

I told her to trust her women's intuition, which would have told her, "Fool, go to sleep". I wanted her to do that but in prayer. When we enter dark places in life, blessings are sure to follow.

She said, "I asked him, 'Honey, why didn't you answer your phone? I spent most of the night and half the morning looking for you. I even rode around thinking I could spot your car.'"

She said that his answer were vague, and the look on his face said, all he wanted was sleep and to be left alone. I felt her pain. I told her that the battle she was fighting wasn't hers but his.

She said, "He was lying on the sofa after being out all night. I asked him, 'Where have you been? Surely, a wife deserves an answer.' She stated, "he started hitting me in my face, head, anywhere he could". He struck me with his fists. I kept telling him to stop."

"Why didn't you fight back?" I asked her.

"I tried to break away, but I guess I was too afraid to say anything or fight back fearing that the abuse would only get worse."

I asked her about the tenants upstairs. I asked her in my thoughts, *How could you be so stupid as to not yell out for help?* I guess she was afraid and embarrassed. I reminded her to pray in all things good and bad; I told her Jesus was always listening and took joy in giving us proper direction.

She's made some life changes for the better. We still talk, her life pain has subsided, she found herself and now offers supports to others. I have a much different pain that we talk about. Jesus is the ruler of all that breathes, the mighty one who never sleeps. He makes the ultimate decisions in our lives. We may choose our actions, but Jesus determines their consequences as he loves and supports us through it all. However, many of us may feel indirectly burdened by others' actions and their consequences. I have learned a new version of unfairness and how it's applied to our world.

It's not the world; it's the people in the world. There is no reasoning; there are only facts and how I perceive this part of my life. Some people just seem to want this world turned upside down. It seems that some people are all about self. What a selfish world it has become. Many women and some men have fallen into the trap of hurting others and making judgments. Many are trapped in believing the words of others without any evidence of their truth. "He (or she) said he loved me," some will say. I say you must love yourself more. God's plan is always different from and better than ours, and God's plan is always waiting for us. He's waiting for us to let go of what's no good for us.

There's no way I could handle being abused by anyone especially someone who said he loved me. I think if I had been my friend in that situation, I would have cried out to Jesus. Maybe she did. I would say, "God, please take me away from the man I love who seems to hate me, by his actions."

Be careful of the battle between the heart and the mind. The heart might try to convince you to stay, but your mind will ask you, *Are you crazy? Get out while you can. Enough is enough!* A man would have to hate something inside himself before he would give up being or becoming the man God destined him to be—a loving, protector, supportive provider for his family as well as himself. Men have power they can use for good or evil. Women have power too that they can use effectively or ignore, thinking they can't change their situation. They must be empowered to use their power effectively to benefit themselves and be examples for other women who feel stuck or ineffectual.

It is never okay to put up with abuse; there's always a door that leads out of that room even if it's pitch-black inside. There's no need for anger when it's so much easier to love. I too wanted my marriage to work. I loved him so much, but it seemed my voice was never heard. I felt broken and unsure of the present and future. As painful and difficult as it was, I had no option but to walk away with tears in my eyes but peace in my heart and God's strength for my upcoming battle. I had no idea that my strength was being tested but also being increased. Tests are a fact of life. My failed marriage was a test; I relied on my strength to execute my decision to be strong in all things, or so I thought.

Just like the pain of my dysfunctional marriage, I prayed that the morning of April 20, 2010, would disappear from all calendars and anything else that displayed that fateful day. I had no idea that my past life storms—broken marriage, incomplete choices—that exhausted me at the time would make me stronger. Many times, I wondered about my faith. *Can I even define it? What is faith? How does it work? How and where do I use it? Does everyone have it?* But I knew I had to demonstrate my faith, knowing from my biblical teachings that faith does not always determine fate. It's also not the amount of faith you have or think you have; it exists in each of us. I had to learn to use it for a lifetime. Faith became my life sentence. What must occur in our lives according to God's plan will occur whether we're ready and willing or not.

As I looked around in the dimness of the room, the only light was coming from the TV. I couldn't tell what program was on. Though my eyes were open, the TV was watching me. I wondered what determined how much I could take. *Who decides how strong I should be and under what circumstances?* I thought about my trials and tribulations. My mind drifted to a dark place I'd become acquainted with, it was an uncomfortable place. It's not necessarily the room or space itself that defines its calmness; it could be the lighting, how the furniture is arranged, the colors of the walls, or the mood an individual perceives in that space or brings into it.

I couldn't find any calmness or peace. I'd searched my mind and heart, yet peace was nowhere to be found. *Where's the peace I so desperately seek? Could it be hiding?* I shrugged and hung my head. I felt mercilessness, seemingly endless pain, and heartache. I closed my eyes and tried to think clearly. I prayed to the Holy Spirit for peace and understanding. *Doesn't the Bible say the Holy Spirit was sent to be our comforter?* I couldn't perceive anything that resembled comfort or peace. I was numb. I couldn't move. My mind was stuck in time—that day, that hour, that moment. My thoughts reminded me that my life was not a dream—it was real and it was mine to live and deal with for better or worse.

My eyes were heavy and filled with tears. I glanced at all the pictures on the wall, especially the pictures of him. My mind was racing with thoughts of things I couldn't change in my current situation, didn't expect in my future, things I'd started but hadn't completed, moments I wish I had captured on my smartphone—a portrait or a video. I realized it wouldn't matter how ugly I looked or what I was wearing, I just wished I had taken more selfies with him. Unimportant things such as parent-teacher conferences became important in hindsight; I wished I had recorded those. How I would have loved to have been nominated for the weirdest parent for taking conference portraits with my smartphone.

I had never thought I'd have to live through times like this. During that terrible storm in my life, I asked myself if it would have been easier just to die. *Why would Jesus allow me to live to see what would break my heart and never leave my thoughts?* Then I asked myself, *If I died, who would help the mothers and families heal? Who would be better to understand loss of a child than another mother, me?* Unfortunately, I had something in common with many of them. *I thank you, Jesus, for allowing me to help others.*

I had to renew my strength to endure another day of despair. I had to believe my anguish wouldn't last forever. I closed my eyes to maintain my focus. *Lord, don't let me lose my mind. Please don't let that thought cross my mind. You have given me a very important mission—to help others, one or a million of them.*

God works all our negative circumstances together for our good. There have been so many days that I thought would never end. Then I wake to a tomorrow I'd like to forget simply because I don't know what to expect, yet somehow, it's found its way into my life repeatedly. There will be some issues I can't change, own, or resolve. They are what they are. Isn't that what some say when they don't have any answers to life's storms?

My heart was so burden and my mind was clouded with the "Why?" feeling. I felt I'd been sent to war with no training, no ammunition—nothing—and had to face my constant enemy, heartache.

My nose flares and my eyes fill with tears now as I reflect on that day and the many tomorrows that followed. I must remember that whether tomorrow is positive or negative, I will always do something to improve it. I might face unwanted challenges and defeats, but I must remember that nothing on earth is perfect and that I will live through those storms as well.

Another great thing about Jesus is he offers us time to recover (smile) and time to heal while living. Honestly, I'm not sure if I'll heal completely in my lifetime. However, I will live each day I open my eyes. I write about the todays and tomorrows that I've had to live through. It's funny that tomorrow becomes my yesterday, and as much as I would like to exclude yesterday, I know that's where all the memories—some good, others bad—are. They're all I have left when I think of my only son. I can live only through each day—each of them will eventually take care of itself.

I know this because in spite of it all, I'm still standing. I stand not alone but with Jesus, who is much stronger than me. He can be the strong tower for anyone or anything. There is no problem he can't solve. Life and painful circumstances can be difficult especially when I attempt to rely on just me. I must not forget that there is a higher power stronger than me, a power with perfect timing in all situations—Jesus.

I remain in contact with some of my son's friends. They know things about him, I don't or can't remember. I love listening to those old stories and jokes they share. How I wish I were there so I could revisit them now. I can visualize them because they are told in such detail. Some of them make me happy; others cause me to smile. My smile is a disguise to cover my pain so I don't cry in my anger and confusion.

When I'm alone, I revisit the times I shared with him because I don't want to forget anything about him. I remember them by keeping my focus on the happy memories; the sad memories only remind me of how sad things became. I asked the Lord, *Perhaps you have me confused with someone else?* Then there's the *Why me? I'm not the strong one. I'm not prepared for this journey. Truth is I could never be prepared.*

Chapter 2

Storm

Though I hadn't had an appetite for days, I tried to eat just to keep my strength up. My body had forgotten the feeling of hunger. *If my son isn't eating, then why should I?* My mind was consumed with many painful thoughts. My eyes, regardless if opened or closed, could still visualize the pain that he and I both had to endure. The pain of never seeing each other as we had before, my pain remained. *What in God's name were they thinking? What was he thinking? Who's accountable for what I'll have to go through for the rest of my life? Do I suck it up and take the blame for it all?* I had taught him to treat others the way he expected others to treat him, to choose friends wisely, and most important, to stay out of harm's way.

I don't understand many actions of the people in the world today. Many have turned cold and selfish and think only of themselves while chanting, "I got your back." "Black lives matter". That couldn't be further from the truth. How can we live and not want the same for our fellow sisters and brothers? How do we deliver harm and wake the next day and say, "I slept well last night"? How can we fist bump one another and trust no one.

I was trying to make sense of a misunderstood situation. *How do I get through to the human race and make a difference, especially for mothers?* I could have pulled my hair out one strand at a time. I was so angry that I wanted to chew and spit out everything that hurt me, things I'd been robbed of by those secret people-murderers. They had caused me to feel all this unneeded and unwanted pain. I was wounded. I had the scars in my heart to prove it. Anyone looking into my eyes could have seen my soul. A storm that hadn't been in any forecast had occurred. My shirt was moist in the area where my heart was, and there was a puddle of tears at my feet.

Those tears had fallen each time I thought, *I could have changed God's plan.* I had to go on in spite of it all. Maybe those who had caused my pain hadn't realized how my life would be affected. Perhaps they will. Perhaps they just didn't care. The damage had been done. So many lives were affected—mine, his grandparents, and Lord, I can't forget his children. I didn't know what impact he would have been in their lives, but I sure wished he had the chance. Many of his children never knew of him in life, must now or one day make a choice, to love him for the father they imagined him to be or hate him for the father he wasn't to many of them. The murderers had inflicted pain on me for reasons I didn't understand. *Did it change their lives for the better? What is the value of life when it's not your own? Why don't people care about others' lives?* It seemed that hate had come easily for them. They had done it and had just walked away, not worried about the effect of their hatred on others. Those secret people were hiding from the results of their actions. That's just what they did; that was how they got down. They hurt innocent people not thinking of the domino effect.

Lord, please don't forget all the poor mothers, including me, Lord, who will have to live with the results of those secret people's deeds. I had never thought this would be a part of my journey. Who knows which path that has been destined for each of us? As the Bible says, no one knows the day or the hour, but that's true for many events in life, not just death. All I could do was ask for strength.

Certain days, I believe I have it all figured out—the cause and effect of a situation. Other days, I ask myself, *Why's this happening?* I was taught never to question God, who knows what's best for us. When the timing is bad, my understanding becomes diminished and denial kicks in. My last real storm in life destroyed almost everything inside me; the only things viable were my heart and mind; they somehow survived the denial, emptiness, anger, mood swings, outburst, withdrawals, depression, and pain. It's been difficult to believe it's good for me (smh— shaking my head). Then I remember that God never said life would be easy. We all have our own definition of easy, but we can all survive our storms. At times, I want to hide from life's storms and shout, "Go pick on someone else!" Those are the storms that make me cry because there's nowhere to hide; I have to face them. I had to face the reality that he is no longer here in the flesh.

At this moment of sharing my innermost feelings, I'm hitting the computer keys with force because I'm angry, hurt, and mad as hell. It's not easy to share my feelings because my heart has been weakened and seems to be always under construction. In spite of all the pain I've been through, God has proven that it's possible to rebuild and regain strength when we talk about what seems too big to handle alone. We must believe in his power and speak good into existence. I would like to personally thank you, reader, for allowing me to vent into your perhaps busy schedule.

The acceptance of life's painful changes is sometimes harder than going through the storm of life itself. Well, here come those thoughts again, those painful thoughts of the day my life changed. I can't keep them to myself. They're too much at times. *Please let me cry out*, I think. I opened my mouth, but the only sound that's heard is dead silence. The sound of my voice can't be heard because I'm trying to put on my big-girl panties; it's so hard not to cry when the pain is so deep.

Who in their right mind would allow a mother to cry out for her child due to a tragic event that could have been prevented? I could have been used those tears for another storm in this confused and often heartless world. The silent cries are the loudest because the inside of your heart can become so full of pain that it feels like it's about to burst. My heart filled with pain continues to like the rise of the sun—every day.

In my pain, I must remember to pray so Jesus' angels will surround, protect and grant me peace in the knowledge that in spite of it all, I'm okay and never alone. I know firsthand that denial prevents the mind from receiving the happiness, God offers to all who will allow it in. This too is a human skill that is gained with patience and desire.

Chapter 3

Strength

Jesus, where are you and your stripes by which I can be healed? Where is the helm of your garment? I want to touch it. I don't have an issue of blood, but my heart is bleeding. Does that count for anything? I'm dying inside, and no one but you, me, and most mothers who are living with a broken heart understand that. Can you see our tears? Can you hear our hearts skipping beats? Lord, please continue to teach us to live while healing. Let our bleeding hearts be payment enough. I know you never said it would be easy, but I never thought it would be so hard.

I'm so angry because I wasn't prepared for this storm. Lord, you've given me a challenge I'm not sure I have the mental and physical capacity to take on. Yet in my heart, I know I must try to live while healing in spite of everything.

Mothers, please let me take your hand as you take mine. Let me carry your storm on my shoulders today. I'm willing to stand in the gap for you. I share your pain; I know it all too well. I also believe that through pain we can develop strength.

I am willing to stand in the gap with you and for you no matter how difficult the challenge, no matter how long it takes, or how many you are. God has sent me to help as many of you as I can. One or a million, every one of you are important. I will help aloud by yelling out for you in prayer. I will help in the silence of my mind. I will beg God to heal us because I am aware that many of you may not understand what "It's all for our good" could mean. How does good feel so bad? I'm smh—shaking my head, I continue to share this thought with you. I will cry out sharing my tears and mixing them with yours.

There might be a day when you're exhausted from crying and weak from the physical or mental pain of life's sometimes crooked path of losing children that God loaned to us. I'm here in silence with my head bowed, hands together, and eyes closed. The only sounds are the skipping beats of my broken heart. I hope you will find peace if only for a moment; that's in the best interests of your heart and your health. Take a deep breath; continue to live. I'm not saying move forward and forget the past; I'm saying don't give up in spite of it all. We can live while we heal.

I do that by not losing focus on the power of the strength that surrounds me. A small mustard seed of faith. God's strength won't allow me to fail in overcoming any challenge. My patience and his timing go hand in hand. Mothers' remember I'm here always in prayer. When it comes to the broken heart of a mother, nationality and language might differ, but heartache is universal.

As I cry for myself and others, my tears are warm yet my soul feels cold. So much has changed since April 20, 2010. I can respond so negatively; I'm so angry sometimes at anything, anyone, for any reason. I want mothers to know that it's okay to be angry not because I've been but because often people think that everything will be fine in time. Some say time will heal. I ask, "On whose watch?" Time often stands still, but I move forward. That's what he would have wanted, right? I close my eyes to escape the pain and confusion in my mind, but my homeless heart can feel it all. It's like being on a roller-coaster. Once at the top, we hold on tight and close our eyes hoping everything will turn out fine. Hard, soft, fast, or slow, we can't prevent the fall or determine the outcome.

Mothers, if we could pick our storms, our forecasts would call for warm, sunny days with only intermittent rain showers. And we must believe God's umbrellas can withstand any storm.

Chapter *4*

Trust

I t happened years ago, yet it feels as if I just received that unwanted call, you know the call that pops up on the caller ID you don't want to answer, the call that has you respond, "I don't think I know that number."

It could also be the call that pulls your heart down into your stomach and gives you overwhelming anxiety that can't be prayed away. You're afraid something could be dreadfully wrong. Many can relate to that; others should pray it never happens to them or their loved ones. Some might say, "I can't believe it. Things like this happen only to other people." Some might think or even dare to say, "God hates me! No one else is going through this. How can he be so mean? Why won't he protect me? Where's your mercy, Lord?"

My countless prayers seemed useless. I had hoped to reminisce with family and friends of how things were and how I thought things would be now. Then I had to face the reality of what was and what would be. God's will is always done his way at his time; I guess that's why it's called long-suffering. Unfortunately, we have no control over how long our suffering will last or how bad it will be; that's all up to God. It's not in our hands. I could feel my suffering deep down in my soul as I cried out, "Jesus! Please help me. I can't help myself! You are the maker and ruler of all, so please allow my prayers to come true and put the enemy beneath my feet so I can walk in peace and joy. Lord there's no time for a life storm. The timing is all bad. I just can't do this now. Not now, please, I beg you!"

Then I realize I'm doing what I said I couldn't do—I'm facing one of my greatest fears. I'm trying to understand this craziness.

"Jesus, where are you? I thought you were always on time. I need you now. I need you like yesterday. I'm sorry,

Jesus, I'm so angry. Lord, why are you picking on me? Can't you see all that I'm going through including my broken marriage? Lord, no one understands, but how can I expect anyone to understand what I myself know nothing about? I believe I have faith. I've been taught about your mighty and endless power. I know if anyone can perform a miracle, it's you. Lord Jesus, please fix it—make the pain go away. I'm not sure I can hold it all together."

Some people lose their minds, become withdrawn, or self-medicate, turning to drugs and alcohol but discover is a temporary fix or a lifetime problem. Some ask, "Who is this Jesus? I've never heard of him. If he's so wonderful and all-knowing, why does he let bad into a good life?" Others think they control their destinies without realizing that's not true; God chooses us for particular tasks at different times. Same with our battles—God orchestrates them all.

It didn't matter how many times I was reassured that everything would work out just as planned by God; the unbearable pain never left. It took my breath away; it changed me. My laughter became shorter, less human—not animalistic but less meaningful. I'd often thought I was a good person who treated others well. *Why me?* I asked. I heard the Holy Spirit ask what my ears didn't want to hear and my mind still says, *Why not you?*

With tears in my eyes and heaviness in my heart, I was consumed. I looked in the mirror and asked myself, *What makes you so special?* The thought made me shake my head in disbelief. God loves each of us. It doesn't matter who we are, who are children are, the color of our skin, sexual preference, religion, or lifestyle. It doesn't matter what we go through, been through, are currently enduring, or what we may not have gone through yet. What matters is our ability to withstand the storms, the unknown.

I'm learning to trust the life and circumstances of the unknown. Just as each of us is different, God's plans for us are different. His mighty power can unexpectedly change our direction in a blink of an eye. It's up to us to follow a sometimes difficult path or just selfishly throw in the towel and pursue life whatever his will suggests. The unknown path he might put us on could increase our ability to help others in need of prayer or support.

We must remain strong in our faith in God and his ability to help us even when we can't understand uncomfortable changes in life. We must recognize our inability to help ourselves and withstand what we don't understand. Mothers, my help comes from above every day.

I don't think life will ever be easy; it's a work in progress, but it can be made easier if we lean on God, not ourselves or the world. When we know better, we should do better. We have to open our mind and eyes to see God's unchanging hands.

The world will offer its opinions but lack solutions for situations that need to be experienced. When it comes to those real-life situations that hit home, we should rely on the Lord. "Lord, I'm waiting on you because you have the power to make what's hard easy. Lord, I know you can help me realize that you're always right and on time. You can surround me with what or whomever I need. You can protect me against whatever challenges my faith when I feel like a victim of circumstance. Lord, please stay with me and keep me strong. When the world can't or won't offer me the hope and peace I need, I let my belief and faith in you surpass it all."

Chapter 5

Faith

I often ask, "Why so much pain, and why me, Lord? Are other mothers under attack? Is it incident or accident of an individual's thoughtless actions that result in such destruction that the mothers pay with their hearts for life?"

It could be that the children of the chosen mothers are being sacrificed for the glory of God. Mothers' remember to be aware that he can see all. The reward for strength is priceless. I too am onc of those mothers who have been penalized without cause. Please don't feel alone; I am here also. I was chosen to make the ultimate sacrifice of my son. I don't say that to receive pity; other mothers have lost much more. I say it to remind myself I am strong in the arms of God; he will comfort me in my sacrifice chosen by him.

Some people think they see clearly but lack understanding of what surrounds them. They don't seem to recognize the effects of what they perceive as right because they don't care to think about the effects it will have on others. My sacrifice changed my life for the better and for the worse. They sure didn't think of me or my son on April 20, 2010. They reacted without a plan. They couldn't have had one; if they had, my heart would be filled with joy. Maybe I didn't look at that day as they did. They looked from their eyes with blurred vision. The vision of today is, "Here and now—no one matters but me." They must not have seen correctly and didn't realize they were handing me a death sentence too. I wish they had thought of mothers just for a second.

That day, their eyes must have been filled with hatred for my son based on the way he looked or didn't look, what he had, or they thought he had, what he did or didn't do. I still don't know if it was personal. I do know it was already written in the book of life. Most of my son's life was good. As my uncle would say, "Don't dislike me—get like me." I have many times wondered about the violence in this beautiful world created by God. Have we as the human race turned something so beautiful into a hot mess?

Having blurred vision is a choice, not a part of life. I pray that my vision will not be blurred to the pain of the world; I want to better understand my God and how I can learn to trust knowing he won't put more on me than I can bear/endure. At times, I struggle with what I think is too much, but I ask God to help me, to be my strength and shield. So that I can become the best part of me. I'm thankful he surrounds me.

Mothers' know that if he helped me, he can help you also. God is just and fair in all he does. He has no one chosen person—not you, not me. Blink so your vision can be cleared, your mind will be alert, and your strength will be renewed; life isn't over until you can no longer feel the earth beneath your feet or the wind on your skin.

The strength to believe and understand is simply being willing to be there for someone else during his or her storms. God makes the sun shine even through the rain. We must use our hidden strength to offer a shoulder for others to cry on. God is strong when we're weak. We must be prepared for life's unwanted and unusual storms. There is always something deep inside us that we don't have a clue about. It happens just when we think all or most of our life struggles have been justified to God. This storm occurs sometimes, without warning—no help, no best friend. At times, we'll think we don't have what it takes to be effective for anyone, not even ourselves. We must remember that there's so much power in us we haven't tapped into because we don't think we can utilize it, we think it doesn't exist, or we think we've already used it up.

Prayer changes things if we are willing to believe in its power, be patient, and understand the will of God and all his promises. God cannot and will not lie to us; he loves us even when it feels he hates us. He will never leave us or forsake us because he loves us today, tomorrow, and forever.

Chapter 6

Hope

I have experienced heartache and fear. Many times, I wasn't sure how I would survive; at those times, I had to use my inner ability to fight my problems or flee them. Here's my analogy of what occurred that changed my future.

On April 20, 2010, my cell rang on God's orders. I couldn't flee; I had to endure whatever it was. This battle belonged to me, Felicia. We can choose to do nothing, or we can verbally and mentally fight back when we're engaged in a battle. Sometimes, it's not about us but about God for his glory and the demonstration of his power.

I decided to fight. How could I run from anything associated with me? I know my son is counting on me to make sure his story is told and his now silent voice is heard. I too want him to know how much I love him (tears, tears, tears).

Mothers, I want to help you; perhaps you'll obtain the skills, will, and courage to help yourself and others. Most important, you might need to be the voice of a closed mouth.

I loved my son unconditionally, as he loved me. I loved his smile, laughter, jokes, compliments, kisses, and the love we shared.

"God, you knowing this and me believing in you for most everything in my life, what happened, dear Lord? Please hear my cry. What did I do wrong? I'm not perfect. I know that without a doubt."

I thought I had it all together. I would listen carefully to everyone, and I had answers for almost everyone. I'd graduated from college, provided a comfortable living for my family, and didn't have many days when food was less than adequate.

I raised three children—Damond, my son, and Yasmina and Kerissa, my daughters—for the most part alone. It didn't matter whether I was married or not; I always felt I was a single parent. I had been married and experienced pain when that relationship failed in spite of my efforts to make it succeed.

Mothers, remember that we share all our experiences with our children even when they grow up and become adults. I vowed not be so consumed with breakups and mishaps in my life that I would leave my "post" as mother, a post I consider priceless. The choices I made and their results taught me to be a better mother and person and to teach others by my example.

Motherhood doesn't come with instructions; we learn as we live. I define my mothering as laid back but firm when needed. My children tell me now that I was too lenient with them at times. I love them unconditionally. I did punish them at times, but it was always to correct their behavior. At times, my parenting was wrong, but I always tried hard to be a good mother to them. I experienced love, happiness, laugher, and commitment as a mother, and I have good memories.

Most of all, I experienced God, who became my foundation. He taught me to be hopeful while living in a world that could leave me in doubt and despair. I've become a stronger and better me, grandmother, mother, and advocate. I didn't realize that transformation was possible. God isn't like us. He is perfect in his thinking, timing, and constructing our beings. His plans for us were in place before the beginning of time.

I learned that God had my back. I did the best I could for my kids and myself. I made many decisions—some good, some bad—but they were all mine. The Lord stuck by me. No, my wrongs weren't made right in an instant, but unknowingly, I became stronger. Tragedies can strengthen us and teach us to handle life's next challenge or to help others when they need it.

Chapter 7

Love

I am an only child raised by a single mother and grandmother I look up to. My mother, Addie, a.k.a. Penny, has always been filled with strength, love, and determination even though she lives with a broken heart herself. She had been diagnosed with cancer and thanks to God she is now in remission. At times when I wanted to talk about the pain we shared, with the loss of my son, she'd change the subject. She'd say, "If I think about it too long, I'm afraid I'll start screaming and never stop, run, and never fall." It's easier for her to bury her painful thoughts and not talk about them. I respect her decision, but I often wonder how difficult it must be to live with all the pain she holds inside.

As I was growing up, I went to many good schools and always had a comfortable home. From a child's perspective, my life was the best ever. I was only a teenager when I became pregnant with Damond Jermaine Richard Lavell Harris; yes, he had three middle names. Jermaine was one of the Jackson Five. I laugh at the thought of being one of their many fans. Richard was in honor of my late father, and Lavell was my favorite uncle's middle name.

Damond loved bragging especially to girls about his many names. I believe he used those names to either impress them or identify them by which name they used when calling him. My mother and grandmother nicknamed him Money. I don't know how he got that name, but that's what everyone called him, and in his later years, he had a lot of money. He adopted the nickname Bud (which he stole from a teenage friend), then Face, Mr. Face, and King Face, all based on the rapper Scarface, which became his signature that some tattooed on their bodies.

My son loved the song "Smile"; he played that song so much that I think he thought he was Scarface himself (lol). Damond does resemble him. My mother and grandmother took on the primary responsibility of raising him as I was just a kid myself, a teenager.

Chapter 8

Shattered Belief

At first, as many mothers would be, my mom was very upset about my pregnancy. How could I blame her? I was only fourteen and didn't have a clue about raising a child or how I had conceived him. At that tender age, I didn't know what sex was; it was my first time. I had ended up in a bed wondering what I was doing there and what was coming. It was painful. No one foresaw the great blessing that would enter humanity and would change so many lives including mine. I thank God for my family's help and support.

My mother and I found out I was pregnant when my endless sleeping and fatigue prompted her to seek medical attention for me. Everyone was shocked, most of all me. *Pregnant? A baby? What's going on?* I hadn't mastered being a teen. How was I supposed to know anything about the trouble it seemed I'd unknowingly gotten myself into? How could I have known that one decision would change my life?

My mother was devastated. My grandmother's first response was, "She should have an abortion," but my mother wouldn't allow that; she had a strong love for children and wanted more after I'd been conceived, but God had blessed her with only me. I say that with a big smile; she's a rare diamond, priceless to me.

We got through it with God's mercy. He can always see what we can't; he knows what's to come and how to prepare us for victory. God is the father; he knows best. He is the eternal Alpha and Omega.

I lived with my late, loving grandmother Dorothy (on my late father's side) for a time prior to Damond's birth. I guess that was the best decision for everyone; we all needed to adjust to this life-changing experience. On May 11, 1976, my child was born premature—four pounds thirteen ounces—but healthy and strong. He was welcomed with more love and open arms than any child could want or dream of.

My grandmother was so nervous because he was so small; she made sure we carried him around on a pillow so no one would break him (lol). She was so loving and caring to everyone, including Damond. Grandma gave him his nickname Money and used that for him exclusively.

But I didn't think of motherhood and parenting; I was very young. Many adults find themselves in a similar situation when they become parents; adulthood doesn't endow anyone with the ability to be a parent. Life can be so complicated that some things pass us by—things we can't redo and things we forget to place in our hearts. Second chances may have boundaries; sometimes, they never occur, and sometimes, they become a memory of what we wish we could do over.

Those chances may also come with a price that may take a lifetime to redeem ourselves from. If only we could think of everything and write it in our hearts and minds in hopes of no regret, no shame, and no doubt. We must first remember that we are only humans and prone to make mistakes we can't fix. I've looked at things I've handled and asked myself, *Could I have done that in a better way? Should I have made a different decision?* I can worry enough that I forget joy comes in the morning, forget to be patient, and forget to use my strength to see me through. I can feel mentally and physically paralyzed in a world I once knew well. What were identifiable as love and peace are hidden by hate and war not between countries but between people who act one way but think another when dealing with people who aren't two-faced as they are. How can I make a painful situation less painful when it's already as painful as it can be?

I've asked myself plenty of the what ifs: *Could I have …? Why didn't I say …?* It's never too late to change our lives' quality no matter the quantity of our heartaches. Many times, I thought I was too late to change my situation for the better, and other times, I had to accept what I couldn't change. I remember being sent to a school on Milwaukee's north side for young expectant mothers. I thought my mother would never get over that. As my months of pregnancy progressed, I was diagnosed with blood poisoning, which could have been fatal, but that wasn't God's plan.

I was admitted to Mount Sinai Hospital and had a C-section. One day, I was an innocent child, and the next, I was a curious teen who thought she knew it all but learned that wasn't the case. You may not know how you got to where you are, but if it's an uncomfortable place, remember that even when you're weak, God is strong.

Whenever I feel weak, I reach in my soul and ask for the strength I need. Many have family, friends, and others they can lean on for strength, but at times, there are limits to the help they can offer due to their commitments, circumstances, and abilities. Some might not realize others are in need of support. People will let you vent, but that doesn't mean they really know how you feel. I think it's easier when their response is, "It will be okay. Time will heal." At times, I felt alone and abandoned by those who had said they were my friends but didn't act that way. I will own my truth; I changed; I didn't take it all personally. Please remember, mothers, to pray for your minds; ask God to grant you peace if you need it.

I also have friends who love me and were present as often as possible; their timing was perfect. I had two very special friends who died during my life storm. Both I had known for many years. I shared most everything with one of them (smile). However, due to her physical and mental challenges, she was unable to verbally offer her love and support she was once known for. Rest in heavenly peace, my friends. Their deaths made my storm intense. I asked God, "How could you allow me to lose them now? Can't you see I'm going through a storm right now? Lord, I don't need this type of boundary. What I need is my friends." Then I tried to get my emotions in check so I could think clearly.

We need boundaries in life so we can grow in our understanding of what our minds can't comprehend. Many tell those going through difficult times, "You look well! I'd have never known what you've been through." They can be surprised to hear in response, "It's not as easy as it looks. I'm really hoping for better days." At times, all I can do is be thankful for enough strength to withstand another day.

Once, the Holy Spirit encouraged me to pray. I asked, "Pray? For whom? My ex? He hurt me badly." At that time, I was in so much pain. My first reaction was "No!" But in my soul, I wanted to do the right thing, so I begin to pray in spite of it all. "Lord, please save him with your blood. Because no matter our past, the most important thing for all people is the salvation you offer to those who believe in you, trust you, and want salvation."

I could feel the Holy Spirit as much as I could feel the air I breathed. "Pray for your children," he said.

"My children?" I asked. "You must be wrong, at least this time. Maybe you have the wrong Felicia. My children are healthy and young; they have their whole lives ahead of them."

But I knew the Holy Spirit was there to comfort me. I knew the voice of the higher power. It's difficult when you have to listen to something that isn't music to your ears. I thought he was giving me a warning before a storm. *My last days might be near. I'll prepare, get things in order.* "You can't be right! Not my children!" I knew God doesn't give us the spirit of fear, but I was terrified. I prayed for my children, mother, grandmother, friends, ex-husband, and even my unknown enemies. I felt hopeless and desperate. I prayed for myself; I wanted to make sure heaven would be my destination. I was sure Jesus had died for us and our salvation.

We all can be saved; heaven can be our final destination no matter what our storms in life are. What's most important is that we face them without fear because God does not give us the spirit of fear; rather, he gives us the ability to face our storms with faith and determination. We must believe that whatever God does in our painful situations will be a blessing in disguise even if at the time we're in tears, as angry as can be, or in great pain.

It all happened so quickly on April 20, 2010, a Tuesday. I put a towel over my phone and turned the ringer off. So I wouldn't be distracted when I was working out on my treadmill at the gym. I was determined to make that workout session count; I had a few pounds to lose.

About thirty minutes into my workout, I lifted the towel and glanced at my phone. I saw that I had gotten some calls from Chicago, where my son lived. *Dear God in heaven.* I listened to one message: "This is Stroger Hospital in Illinois. I'm looking for Felicia Noble, the mother of

Damond Harris …" I hung up on the message and called the number. I was shaking. The person who answered asked me to confirm who I was in relation to Damond.

"Where's my son? Why are you calling me?" I asked.

"Your son has been in an accident."

I begged my mind and heart not to think the worst but to think positively and have faith.

"He's in surgery."

"Surgery? Why? What type of accident was it?"

"Where are you?"

"Tell me about the accident! What happened? Did you speak to him?"

"Did you say you're in Milwaukee?"

The adrenaline was racing through my veins. No one could hear my screams. *Am I dreaming?* "Please have the chaplain see him!" The most important thing was his salvation.

I continued to plead for answers. "An accident? What type of accident?" I knew he was a fast driver, but then I also remembered his diabetes and the difficulty he had had adjusting to that.

"He's been shot."

"Shot where?"

"In his leg."

"As in his femur? He could bleed out!"

"Are you coming? Will anyone come with you?"

"I'm on my way!"

I was running a race and was already losing. *Am I in a real-life nightmare?* I passed others in the gym and said in disbelief, "My son has been shot!" I jumped in my car, which my son had given me just months prior. I called a coworker with the news and asked her to start praying. I called my roommate. "I'm on my way to Chicago. I need you to go with me. I don't know my way to the hospital in Chicago. Damond has been shot. I need to get to the hospital."

As I was driving, I spotted my oldest daughter, Yasmina. I stopped, got out, and took off my sweaty workout clothes right in the street. I was standing in nothing but my underwear. I couldn't believe it—my son shot three weeks before his birthday. *Not my son!* I put on my dry clothes. My daughter began to pray. I began to stutter. I called my roommate, "Wh—wh—where are you?"

"I'm near. I see you."

I jumped in their car, and we headed to Chicago. I would have called Brenda, my best friend for over twenty years, but she was very ill and couldn't respond (tears, tears). *I really need her, Lord.* I guessed it was another time Jesus wanted me to depend on just him.

As we drove, the phone kept ringing; everyone had heard the news. My stuttering continued. I hadn't been to many areas in Chicago. I was depending on Patrick, the driver, who had been born and raised in Chicago. It was the longest ride I've ever taken. The traffic was bumper to bumper. *OMG.* I looked at Patrick, who was avoiding eye contact. "D—d—do you know where you're going? If you don't ge—get me to that hospital quick, I'm gon— going to hit you upside your head." Dead silence. *What am I doing here? What in the hell is going on? We're still bumper to bumper. I hope we're not lost.*

Finally, we arrived at the hospital; I jumped out as soon as Patrick parked. I rushed to the unit where I longed to see my son. Several medical staff approached me as if they had been expecting me. I fell to my knees. A doctor asked, "Are you the mother of Damond Harris?"

"Ye—ye—yes." My spirit was shattered. With just my eyes, I asked him, *Where's my son?* The doctor lowered his head and shook it. I asked, "Did you try to save him? Are you a good doctor? Did you do everything you could in the way you were taught?" He responded yes. All I could do was raise my hands. God as always had made his decision. Without warning, no vote required—just his final word.

A nurse asked, "Would you like to see him? We kept him here so you wouldn't have to go down to the morgue."

I managed to rise and walk into the room where my son lay on a gurney. I wasn't the only person in the room, but I felt all alone. I looked at him. He had tape on his eyes. I saw the abrasion on his forehead he had received when he fell after the shooting. I saw blood still draining from his nostrils from the trauma he had endured. I asked the nurse to please remove the tape. I filled a basin with water, grabbed a washcloth, and cleaned his face. My eyes were heavy with tears. "Mama's not mad at you. Mama loves you. It's okay." I kissed him. "Thank you, daughter, for reminding him and he had agreed Jesus is king and that no matter your life's journey, salvation is the road on which to travel. I want to thank you, son, for surrendering to our God, the only one we can all count on in spite of it all."

I remained with my son as long as I could. I looked at him not believing I was standing there and he was lying there motionless. *Dear Jesus, please remind me how to pray. Demonstrate your power. I'm so weak. I need your strength. I have none of my own. Lord why has the world become so cold and mean. Are some people just mad or naw?*

The next day, I left Chicago, but Chicago never left me. That day is etched on my heart. I don't know what all happened that fateful day, but it changed my life forever. I learned that no matter how we look at life's circumstances and outcomes, God has never made a mistake. I had been chosen. I'm happy to stand in the gap. I'm proud to be a voice for the cry of another mother.

Now that some time has passed. I thought my life was beginning to look up when I renewed my relationship with my grandson Sir' Lawrence.

It was years after Damonds' death when he began to develop an unbreakable bond with me. The spitting image of his father, mannerism everything. I'd miss so much time with him. It was a joy to have him in my life. He gave me a sense of peace, a kind of "new beginning". I tried to teach him the morals of life, and what it meant to be a young black man in America. I made several efforts, reminding him not to trust the actions of others. Unknowingly our time together would be brief. He was only twenty with the mind of a young black man trying to find his place in this world. How was he to know that hate was lurking in the air he breathed.

I needed anyone that was a part of my son. As our relationship began to grow. The Lord spoke to me once again. "Felicia it won't be long" I asked myself, what does that mean? What won't be long? After four to six months of spending time together, Sir 'Lawrence was dead, murdered just like his father, my son.

I often remind myself that Jesus is strength how else am I able to withstand this pain. As he does for me he will without a doubt do the same for you.

September 15, 2020 I was getting prepared for bed and I received an alarming phone call "mama DasJon got shot". My heart was pounding in my chest. I fell into the closet as I frantically dressed. I yelled out in prayer "Dear God Dear God". I got to the hospital as quickly as I could. My daughter pacing and screaming. We're in Covid season, no one is allowed in the hospital. Not to mention we've already been informed that he hasn't said a word or opened his eyes. My grandson is only fifteen years old. His mother has his chrome book and all his materials ready for school. Lord don't you remember he just asked me during our summer vacation if I would help him with his homework. "I said yes".

A few weeks prior DasJon called and asked if he could go on summer vacation with us. I said yes and remember to be on your best behavior. He did just that, he made me so proud. Such great memories he had a chance for once not to worry and just be a kid.

After waiting in the parking lot for hours we were instructed to go to another hospital. So that he could have a chance of survival. We arrived and stayed there for hours. The social worker asked Krissy if she would like to come into be with him. The only success of that surgery is that he made it through it. This was a terrible time for everyone. Dasjon passed away on September 16, 2020.

Another grandson dead due to gun violence. Jesus I'm happy you have the wheel because I was about to crash.

I had to be strong for my children and grandchildren and I was. The death of them (Damond, Sir Lawrence and Dasjon) will forever be heavy in my heart. I think of them often. I have endured and I am here for you my friend. I have remained strong in spite of it all.

My Letters

Letter to Jesus

Dear Jesus,

As I begin my notes of thanks and encouragement, it's an honor to start with you, the Alpha and the Omega, the first and the last of everything according to the Bible. You have guided me through my journey of writing this book and have equipped me with a sound mind and body to choose the correct words and tone so your people will learn to manage their lives while healing.

I thank you for being my healer. I know every living thing will ultimately succumb to death. It's all because of your power and plan that was destined before the beginning of time. As your Word says, there are things we must endure until the point of death. Thank you for my strength so I can help others who have lost children. Neither life nor death is possible without you. This I've learned from you, Jesus. Thank you for being my teacher.

Without you, Jesus, where would I be? Thank you for giving me a chance to live in your belief and be alert to your direction and redirection. Thank you so much for allowing me over thirty-three years to be a mother to Damond Jermaine Richard Lavell Harris a.k.a. Mr. Face. It was an honor to raise him with respect for himself and others. At times, he lost his way as many of us do, but he was taught to pray, and he remembered to pray. You gave me parenting skills but allowed me to sometimes make mistakes so I could become a better person and mother. Thank you for salvation, the gift you offer us all knowing we have a choice to accept or reject it. I'm so happy my son accepted your gift of salvation.

The Bible says you chastise those you love; thank you so much for loving me unconditionally yet highlighting my flaws. You remained with me through the good times and the storms. I remember the scripture, "The Lord will never leave nor forsake me." Though many people left me mentally and physically alone when I needed them, I'm not upset because I know the pain I've experienced is new only to me; perhaps it's old to them. Jesus, thank you for being all I need. You, of course knowing all, understand how difficult it's been for me to live without my son. Yes, Lord, I know he is and was always yours; you only loaned him to me. I wish it had been for a longer time, however.

As the tears run down my face, I thank you for the ability to grieve and be angry because of my lack of understanding regarding your timing, which is nothing like mine, but I know it's perfect nonetheless. I appreciate your allowing me to weather this storm. I could not have done any of it had it not been for you. I am not strong enough, but you said that you are strong when I am weak.

Jesus, you are my strong tower, my refuge against any of life's challenge. You're my strength when I had none. Thanks for allowing me to touch so many lives through the words in this book; I have followed your instruction as humbly as I knew how. I don't want to disregard the hearts and feelings of others.

Thank you for prayer, Jesus. I know it changes things. I thanked you often in this letter, Jesus, because you deserve all my praise. You are with me; I know I can count on you because you never tire. Oh how I need you! Thank you for being you. I love you, Jesus. There's no one like you. Bless me, Jesus, as I continue my journey you have made for me.

Letter to My Friends, Coworkers, Inmates, and Patients

I thank you all for caring and listening to my cry. I especially thank Officer Denton for never failing to hug me since the death of my only son. Thank you, Officer Denton, for never being too busy to reach out to me. I knew I could always count on your hugs. I hope you know your hugs gave me so much needed strength.

I know that God put you in my life so I wouldn't lose hope. I couldn't ask for a more dedicated friend. Officer Denton, thank you for never seeming to tire. I felt good knowing that you cared about not only me but also the pain in my heart. When I see you, I feel a few seconds of priceless peace. Your hugs gave me the opportunity to offer my mind some needed freedom.

To all the coworkers who prayed and supported me, you know who you are. I know my mood swings may have been tiresome. I'm sorry. I had never lost a child, and at times, I didn't know how to deal with that. There are days when I still feel I haven't mastered how to hide my pain.

I give a special thanks to the inmates who allowed me to be sad on some days. Thanks for remembering my son's date of birth and death. Thank you for being compassionate and patient with me at a time that was perhaps difficult for you.

Thank you all for inquiring about my well-being and supporting me in the completion of this book, believing in me, and caring, knowing that we are all human and fall short of the glory of God.

I thank the inmates for showing me love and respect and offering me encouraging words. I was able to demonstrate forgiveness, not total hatred, especially to those who had committed the same crime (murder) that took the life of my son.

Mr. Ball, I didn't forget you! Thanks for your warm hugs and remembering my son, your longtime friend. You let me vent and brainstorm my ideas for this book, and you gave me so much love from the very moment God called Damond home. I haven't forgotten your driving me to Chicago to view his body when I was too overwhelmed to do it alone. You were there and remain here always without question. I love you, Mr. Ball. Thank you for the memories and stories that warmed my heart.

Thank you all. I could not have come this far if it hadn't been for all of you. God bless you all.

Letter to My Grandchildren

I want to thank you all for allowing me to be your grandmother. I know there were many times that some of you may not have understood my grief and why I couldn't be the grandmother you may have needed or wanted me to be. I've changed. I'm sorry if I haven't lived up to your expectations. Perhaps you will understand when you're older and more mature that circumstances can change situations and people. I will always love you. I'm happy that my son, your dad, left me with a piece of the fabric—each of you. Please pray for me, and I will pray for you.

I'm sorry if my actions, lack thereof, or harsh words have hurt you. Many times when I was angry … no, that doesn't excuse my behavior. I don't always know how to handle the death of your father. I'm so sorry, grandchildren. I'm living with a broken heart.

He was a great person. He was imperfect, as all of us are. I know he didn't reach out as he should have. I don't know if he knew how. But grandchildren, please believe he loved you all. Don't doubt he didn't want the best for you. Your father is watching you from heaven, and he is with you always (tears).

It wasn't until the last several months of his life that he began to understand fatherhood and its importance. He told me he would ride in the neighborhood where some of you lived to admire you but was too afraid to make his presence known. With ten mothers of ten children, I will accept some of the blame for not acknowledging that you all were in the world. I'm sorry for not teaching my son to be a better father. I too didn't have my father (Richard Richmond, deceased) in the home or in my life.

To the children of my daughters, thank you for your love and support. Help your cousins understand who I really am. I'm requesting this from you because you've always been with me when I'm happy, sad, confused, hurt, and often misunderstood. Yes, Mama Felicia loves you all too. I am proud of all of you.

I thank you for being my grandchildren; it's an honor. God bless you all. Be proud of who you are and your parents and be an example of how to make this world a better place. Don't waste time on unimportant things; stay focused on you and what matters.

Learn to forgive because there will come a time you may need forgiveness. Encourage, support, and pray for each other especially when you don't understand their actions. Be strong, grandchildren, and let the pain of the loss of your father, uncle and cousins remind you that pain and tears make you strong. Remember that negativity is destructive but positivity is explosive. The choice is yours. Strength is best built when you are weak.

Nunu, (Aniyah Alayah and Alaura) Jovonnie, Tyra, Damond, Sir Lawrence (RIP), Kumani, Sa'mour, Tyler, Da'vonn and Da'yania (Damond) Jon'naya, Asianae,

Siniah, and Jeremiah (Yasmina), India, Dasjon (RIP) and Aiyana (RIH) Zion, (Kerissa).

Letter to My Daughters—Kerissa and Yasmina

To my dear daughters, thank you for always believing in me. When my choices were good or bad, you always had my back. You always offered me encouragement, and that gave me assurance to be vulnerable.

I've never doubted that you loved me. Your love cannot be measured. Thank you for supporting me at time of your brother's death and after. That was such a difficult life challenge for us. I'm sorry that was one pain I couldn't fix. I appreciate and am so proud of the women you have become and for raising your children in the best way you know how. Most important, you taught them the priceless lesson that hatred isn't cool. This will be valuable throughout their lives and will result in them becoming people with integrity and respect for others and themselves.

Thank you for keeping my grandchildren, your children, mindful of who I am, not defining me only by my faults and position on the family tree. Thanks for embracing my imperfections; as your brother would say, "Y'all know how mama is—Good looking" (as in agreeing with Damond—lol.

Daughters, thanks for being shoulders I can cry on most any time; I couldn't ask for any better women to call mine. I thank you for allowing me to cry, scream, and yell at you during those times you didn't want to hear it or perhaps didn't deserve it (smile). I'm sorry for sometimes taking my life storm (loss of Damond) out on you. Thanks for embracing my imperfections and being my strong tower when I'm weak.

You both have been great in supporting me—frequent visits to the cemetery, and remembering and identifying my outward expressions of your brother's absence. When I thought no one else loved me, I knew you did. Having your love has always been more than enough. It may be nothing to you, but it's priceless to me. I could never repay you; I wouldn't have made it without you. I ask God to continue to bless you and your families. Damond was so lucky to have you; he couldn't have had two better sisters.

I send this special note, ending with I love you with all my heart. Thank you for everything.

If enough is too much, then what you give is more than enough (smile).

Letter to My Only Son

Well son, I'm not sure how this will go. I'm attempting to hold back tears. Thank you for being my son. You were made perfect for me during the times we didn't see eye to eye—you know, like when you made choices I didn't agree with. I never stop loving you while being proud of who you were. That word *were* is still disturbing to me because it reminds me you're not physically here.

Like many parents, I have so much to hope or pray for. Sometimes, all a mother can do is accept the choices an adult child makes. Son, I've said since you were born—I love you (screaming in agony) and miss you. I've asked God so many times to give you back if only for a short time. I told him so many times everyone said good-bye but not me (shaking my head).

Son, I'm sorry when I failed you. I'm sorry I didn't get to Chicago before the Lord took you home with him. I got there as quickly as I could. I'm so very sorry (tears, tears, tears). Son, I guess I didn't realize just how much I needed you to love, hug, and share new memories with. I thought kids needed parents; I didn't realize how much parents need kids (lol).

I think about the times you protected me by reminding me who you thought wasn't good enough for me. Remembering the time when I was ill (fainting spells) and you called from Chicago in tears making sure I was okay? (Smile). Thank you, son, for caring. You were a great son.

I miss your sense of humor, laughter, and the times I made you angry because of choices I made and how I tried to make sure you were aware when I knew you had my best interests in your heart. I remember when the Holy Spirit began to talk to me; while you and I were in the kitchen, I told you I was sorry if I had ever made you feel I wasn't there for you. You said, "Mama, I forgave you a long time ago" (smile). Thank you for giving me a reason to write and encourage others, especially the mothers, so they will know they're not alone.

Son, continues to rest in peace. As much as I love you, God always loves us more. I often cry for you, but I'm strong. I am your voice. I love you, son. Continue to be blessed, and save a cloud for me. Thank you, son, for being you and for being my angel. Now son I thank and ask that you not only watch over us but Sir and DJ.

A Very Special Letter to Mothers

I thank all the beautiful mothers for taking the time and courage to read my story. I know how difficult it is to reopen wounds. We know some wounds never heal, especially the ones in our hearts. Mothers, let me wrap my arms around you; I'm here with you. I want to walk with you through your journey of losing your child only with your permission. I'm sorry for your loss.

We are a part of the same team, mothers whose hearts ache. We are special and strong though we don't always feel that way. We have been chosen to demonstrate faith and endurance. Mothers' children are dying all around the world. God understands the trials and tribulations we have encountered. Always remember that he loves you.

Don't for a minute think you were singled out even though I did at one time.

Mothers, be proud of who you are and know that there is no perfect mother or person. Don't beat yourself up thinking about all you didn't do and all you could have done. Continue to cherish all you have. You might say to yourself, *I don't have anything, no memorabilia to hold or look at, simply nothing. I just didn't have enough time. I had no idea this was coming.*

Why do children die before their mothers? My answer to that, my precious and strong mothers, is that our children are dying the world over; Jesus has no one favorite person. The time that was given to you and your child is what you were given. It's challenging to live without the one you lost, and yes, people do make bad decisions. Yes, people kill our loved ones not knowing they also kill a part of us. I understand all too well the pain that I too have carried daily. Some mothers' losses are due to illness, but a loss is a loss.

Mothers, stand strong. It won't be easy, but if we stand together, we can manage life while healing by praying, sharing, and encouraging other mothers on their difficult days. Remember as I must that a higher power is always here with us. Please don't take it personally if others—friends and family alike—don't understand the shift in your life; they may have not experienced the death of a child and are unable to comprehend what you're going through.

The Holy Spirit encouraged me to tell you as you know, your child loves you and can easily be found in your heart. I hear your cry. I wrote this book with you in mind. I hope my words keep you encouraged to hold your head up and look up from where your help comes from—heaven.

When your thoughts drift to that unhappy place of your loss, remember to plant a flower of peace so one day it will be a refuge for your heart filled with peace and thoughts that ease your mind. Eventually, you will have a flower garden of beautiful thoughts; you'll be able to close your eyes and smell the sweet fragrance of the Lord and the comfort that the Holy Spirit gives. God bless you all and thank you for your precious time. I will continue to pray for you. I am the cry of another mother.

Letter to Fathers

Fathers, I haven't forgotten about you. I can imagine your heart aches too. I am sorry for your loss. Be strong and assist the mothers in teaching your children the importance of knowing God and his endless power. You will empower them and teach them they can do any positive thing. I'm not pointing the finger at you, fathers; you're the heads of your households, and your sons must be led by your example.

We believe in you and your ability to direct the path of your children, especially our sons. Fathers, as you move forward in your journey, remember that you aren't alone—I'm praying for you. I'm asking God to bless you with wisdom so your teachings will result in change. I know you cry perhaps on the inside; to cry is to heal, and to heal is to gain strength. Remember that where there is a man, there is strength, and where there is strength, there is positive power. This message is sent with love from a mother who can relate to the human heart.

Letter to the Secret People—The Murderers

I write not because of my own personal desire but because I have been instructed to teach the mothers, including myself, to forgive. It seems strange to say "I forgive you" to someone who has robbed me of the most valuable asset a mother could have—her child.

At one time, I hated you although I don't know you or anything about you. Not that any reason is good enough, but you took them away from me/us. I screamed at you so loudly with such force and anger that I could feel the veins pop up in my neck and head. I remember screaming until my voice became hoarse, "I hate you!" I cried like a child who has lost her favorite toy. I realized you couldn't hear me, but I didn't care—I continued to scream as if you could hear every word that came from my mouth. I begged as I asked you aloud and silently, "Why did you have to kill my son? What did he do to you? How did his life affect yours? Didn't you know just how much I loved him? I guess not!"

I hated you because you killed my only son. I don't know what happened that day, but why did it happen?

Why was there so much hate and anger? I came to several conclusions. All this hatred could have been caused by what a person is or isn't—lack of education, employment, support from others friends or family, self-empowerment, and something as simple as love. This has been my observation about many of our young black men. Don't take it personally; it's the observation of one mother with a broken heart. Why else would you kill another human but because of hatred?

Hatred alone is not a reason to take someone's life— you didn't give him his life, so it wasn't yours to take. You were wrong to decide to make us victims—my son and me.

Lord, please help me complete this book (smh— shaking my head). I won't question your instructions, not now.

Secret people, I am still angry at you at times, but to be angry forever would only continue to destroy me physically rather than regain my strength. God says he is strong when I am weak. I thank God he has made me stronger than I could ever have been alone. I thank God he is always here for each of us.

I once thought of all the pain I felt in my heart caused by you. At that moment, I reached for my Bible not looking for any verse in particular. I opened it, and what did I see? The verse that says revenge is not ours but the Lord's. And so I reach into my soul to forgive you because I am in the gap for other mothers and want to be an example of forgiveness to you and others who have made the choice you made. I will not be consumed with bitterness and hatred because my son is not coming back to this world. God has provided him with the peace the world could and would not offer.

I would never want anyone who loves you, secret persons, to feel the pain I do. My forgiveness comes with a price not to you but to me and me alone—the endless pain that remains in my heart. It's my life sentence; it's bittersweet because though it hurts, it has made me strong.

There is no perfect person, including myself. I hope that during the time you've had your physical freedom, you've thought of the changes you can make to be a different person. Please know and remember that violence is never the solution; it only adds to the problem.

The one thing you couldn't take then, and I am not surrendering it now, is my love for him. I forgive you because I want God to be pleased with my obedience. Wherever you are, I pray for peace for your family; I pray they are surrounded with comfort in the storms of life.

I am the cry of another mother. May God bless you, secret person.

Letter to My Mother

Dear Mother,

Thank you for allowing me to bring my son into this world in spite of what many people thought best. Thank you for always being here. It didn't matter if I needed you or not; I was comforted knowing that you are here.

Mom, I know this has been difficult for you. I really hate to see you hurt by something we just didn't have the power to change. You were a wonderful grandmother to them. You did everything right; we couldn't have made it without your guidance. You were like a mother to both myself and Damond. We will always love you, and you deserve so much more.

Your pain has not gone unnoticed; I feel it. Though I haven't witnessed your tears, I know you have cried more than I could ever imagine. Through all of that, you have remained strong in caring for others; yes—lol—that includes me. I know just the thought of them or the mention of their names is unbearable for you. If nothing else, this tragedy has brought you closer to God, and that makes you that much greater in my eyes. What can be better than a mother who fears God? Thank you, Jesus. Mother, I will pray for your continued strength.

I know many of you may share your inner pain only with Jesus, but what better person than him? Remember that Jesus will never bring us to anything he won't bring us through. I love you with all my heart. Damond is watching from heaven, smiling, and thanking you for being his grandmother and always keeping him safe in your heart.

Thank you, Mom, for loving me and unselfishly providing monetary gifts. I know you refuse to take any credit. Jesus and I are very much aware of your kind heart. I have loved you with my whole heart ever since the first day I laid eyes on you—muah! (kiss).

Letter to Reid's New Golden Gate Funeral Home, Milwaukee

I offer a special thanks to Reid's for treating me with royalty at such a tragic time in our family's life. Thank you, Mr. Reid, for all the acts of kindness you and your staff showed me. They have never been forgotten. You covered it all. May God continue to bless you; again, thank you. A special thanks to all who continue to offer support, love, prayer, and words of encouragement. To the Reid family I know that Mr. Reid has gone to be with the Lord. Be blessed. He was so gentle with my love one and my family we are forever grateful.

A Prayer for Sinners

My Father in heaven, I know we are not worthy for your gift of salvation. I have not been obedient to the directions in the Bible. I have broken your laws, and my sins have resulted in me being unable to hear your voice and receive the assistance of the Holy Spirit. You said in Romans 10:9 that if we confess our sins to you and believe you raised Jesus from the dead, we shall be saved.

I am truly sorry. I want to turn away from my sinful ways and get close to you. Please forgive me and help me avoid sinning again. Please help me make choices with a clean heart.

I believe your Son, Jesus Christ, died for my sins, was resurrected from the dead, is very much alive, and hears my cry in prayer. I invite you, Jesus, with open arms to become the Lord of my life. I ask you to rule my life and stay in my heart forever. Please send your Holy Spirit to help me obey you and do your will for the rest of my life. In Jesus' name I pray, amen.

You said in your Holy Word, Romans 10:9 that if we confess the Lord our God and believe in our hearts that God raised Jesus from the dead, we shall be saved.

When I Die

When I die, please don't cry. My Jesus my son and grandsons have been waiting for me high above in the sky. The Lord provided me a good and fair life. In spite of it all, I've lived, loved, and of course for years cried. The tears sometimes exceeded the joy, but it was all in God's plan and for my good—of this you can be sure.

I suffered from chronic heartache because the loss of my child was so difficult to take. I've been waiting for this day. I'd missed my son for so long; now, the wait is finally over and I too am going home. I no longer have to worry and feel the pain in my heart because Jesus is my keeper and has been from the start.

I now have sweet peace, and my soul can rest without falling apart. So think of me or a loved one who has gone to be with our God.

Remember that death is a part of life; it can sometimes be difficult to accept, but take it in stride. Like the dawn, death will eventually be seen by all.

So live, be happy, and sing a few songs. Smile at a stranger and love on a friend; even those good things must come to an end.

This is not good-bye. We will meet again. We will see you above the sky-- God, my son, grandsons and I.

Mothers, be strong. I will pray with the angels from heaven that you will be a little selfish and welcome peace into your heart no matter the storms. So please don't cry when I die. I will be happily reunited with my family above the beautiful blue sky.

* I WAS HER AND SHE IS ME

MEMORIES ARE MADE

Damond 2010 Sir Lawrence 2019 and Dasjon aka DJ

In Loving Memory

Dasjon Riser
"DJ"

Born to Life
January 12, 2005

Born to Eternal Life
August 15, 2020

Printed in the United States
by Baker & Taylor Publisher Services